D1259873

First Practice

Gary Gildner
Storm Lake
April 20, 1971

Gary
Gildner

First practice

University
of
Pittsburgh
Press

Library of Congress Catalog Card Number 72–78533
Manufactured in the United States of America

Acknowledgment is made to the following magazines for poems originally appearing in them: *Antioch Review*, *Epoch*, *Epos*, *Laurel Review*, *The Miscellany*, *motive*, *The Nation*, *Northwest Review*, *Occident*, *Poetry Bag*, *Poetry Northwest*, *Premiere*, *Red Cedar Review*, *Red Clay Reader*, *Sage*, *South and West*, *Tennessee Poetry Journal*, *Wormwood Review*.

for Judy

Contents

I

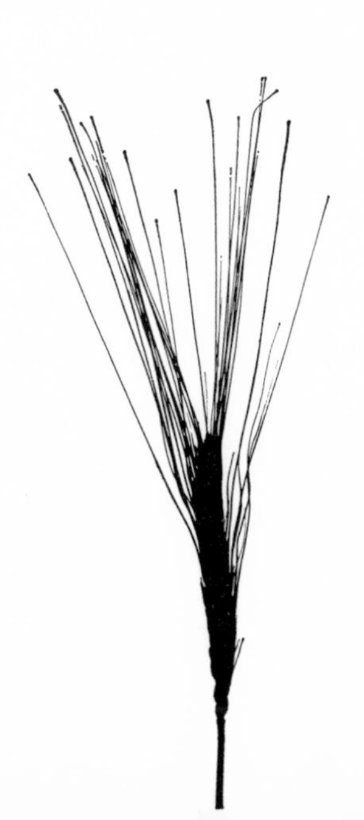

First Practice

After the doctor checked to see
we weren't ruptured,
the man with the short cigar took us
under the grade school,
where we went in case of attack
or storm, and said
he was Clifford Hill, he was
a man who believed dogs
ate dogs, he had once killed
for his country, and if
there were any girls present
for them to leave now.
No one
left. OK, he said, he said I take
that to mean you are hungry
men who hate to lose as much
as I do. OK. Then
he made two lines of us
facing each other,
and across the way, he said,
is the man you hate most
in the world,
and if we are to win
that title I want to see how.
But I don't want to see
any marks when you're dressed,
he said. He said, *Now.*

Under the Hose

We used to run under the hose
when the sun was out,
but when it rained
we ran under the rain—O
it beat a lake by far—
and a pool!—nobody went
to pools. Not Thread Creek Pool
anyway, which was the only pool
we knew about—people
dumped their garbage
in Thread Creek, and once
we heard a headless man
was found all over
the cement chunks they tossed in there
by the bullhead docks—a hillbilly,
some said, from Georgia,
who got in bad with some
colored boys from the North End—
no, we ran under the hose
when the sun was out,
and if it rained, O we
ran like the day you were born!

Stadium Poem

I was sitting alone in the empty Holy
Redeemer High football stadium, smelling
the freshly-cut fat clover I once never had
to fall on—we skinned our shins
and elbows hitting God's good dirt
and liked or lumped it—when I saw a rabbit
hop from the weeds by the hot dog stand
and take a pace that city rabbits take
when there is no rush, to the spot
where I used to kick off before I broke
the bone that did the kicking. It looked good,
eating the grass that was still unmuddied and clean
of blood, and I sat back for a moment filling out
the scene—a stream skimming green moss,
a bed of rocks, the eyes of fourteen deer loose
in the cool dusk, a young bobcat, careful
beside the Yellow Dog Bridge, and several stars, a moon
and leaves until they wouldn't quit . . .

but knowing in the dark piece of my eye
that we pay for escape just the same, I
gathered myself to that spot and waited
—for the leap and press
of a neighborhood tom, giving the night
a single cry, brutal quiet.

April Affair

I woke one morning
and found her curled
as a frightened child
sleeping in the window seat—

beyond her hair
two wrens struggled
with a piece of nest:

in November, on the road to Flint,
I remembered trying to get closer.

Ice Cream Factory

We keep our cool rhythm
under Jack the foreman's nervous fingers:
Pink the fat man mixes the mix
that Angus pours in molds from six
shiny tits, and I work the stick machine
on this dedicated second shift—
a long way from Veblen and Mann,
and the blonde from Cicero
who, at the last minute last spring,
called her body off the ledge
we'd learned to cling to—
but if I don't think about it I'm OK.
Would my friend Ernest say that?—
say push the button, gain your sticks,
lay them neat for Angus
in the mold, in the brine,
in the line that ends where Millie
takes the frozen bars off the racks,
slips on their paper jackets,
packs them in a box for Stan—
who stacks it in the freezer,
puffed up with summer cold?

I say bulky thought, Ernest.
And bulkier still
when the line shuts down at ten o'clock
and everyone goes home.
Everyone, that is, but Millie and Jack—
they'll meet on the sugar sacks;
and the blonde from Cicero,
her hair screaming,
will continue to fall back through space.

For My Sister

You had your nose in a book for years,
accepting academic accolade rather
matter-of-factly: first in your class,
most likely to go on and get your name inscribed
in one distinction after another,
a walking honor-plate of scholarship,
a darling of librarians and nuns and one breed
of mothers—maybe a nun yourself someday, instructing
little ladies how to do extremely well in paper ways,
or perhaps, at some sage age, leading the whole
penguin caboodle through a perfect learned hoop
(shaped of course like a blessed triangle);
but blessed be the Holy Mystery
you got yourself, not a greater bed
of knowledge, but a man instead,
and rather fundamentally instructed him
to pluck the prizes you had tucked away
all the years quite secretly,
in the living, holier place
a little below but above your head.

Rainy Afternoon Between Jobs

I wonder if my mother nine hundred miles away
is sleeping in her room with those three ivory Virgins
and the prayer that glows green in the dark
for the repose of anyone's soul—
if my father is on the sofa, shoeless,
dreaming between the shadows of farm and city
after all these years
and so many hot, sticky weddings, reunions and funerals.

I wonder if my grandmother, having avoided great heights
and all the empty rooms upstairs, has finished
her round of beads and beer and, searching the Gates,
is holding someone's picture, face down, on her knees—
if my friends are getting richer, fatter, or
losing weight too fast, pace the floor alone. I wonder

if the girl who ran away at exactly three o'clock
one Sunday morning clutching the sin to her breast,
leaving behind the pink cashmere sweater,
has thought about us since. And I wonder
if my enemies sitting in the eaves
wonder why I tap the front of my head
against the cool glass, disturbing their afternoon peace.

II

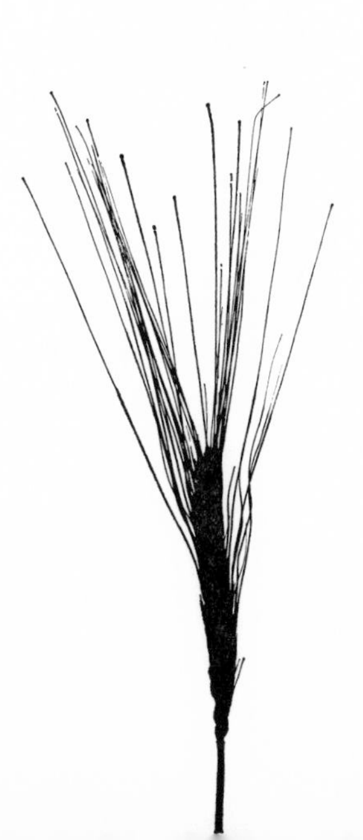

The Shy Roofer

This roofer works at night
on the sly—
he's only a shy man.
Nails, tar, squares covered
and uncovered: these
he proffers quickly,
automatically,
by hand.
It's the moon that's
on his mind, gentlemen—
the stars, the
ladies turning over
one more time
to show their lips,
their honest
hips,
to whisper
in their sleep
you're doing fine,
roofer.

My Coed Wife

My coed wife
reading Lenin
leggy

in her tight red
bathing suit
under

cool water-
colored
pears

is enough
science
for one

afternoon.

Miss Endicotta T. Briskett

Miss Endicotta T. Briskett, fifty-three,
who went to the State University every summer off
and on for twenty years to keep up her teaching eligibility
(she had all six grades in Rock County School since '31—
or from the day her father,

old Sam T. Briskett,
ran off young Albert Cook with a gun
for reading Miss Endicotta Edna Millay): was taken back—
Oh my!—the summer of '64 when in the classroom door
walked her instructor,

to sigh, pointing out the window,
"That pure blue sky, that mellow sun, those miraculous fat
birds—why I believe this day is Heaven-sent!
Now tell me, do you think of Wordsworth? Thoreau? Or"—
and he bent a strange

cool eye toward them—
"are you thinking, 'Gee, I wonder if I'm pregnant!' "
Well. Miss Endicotta T. Briskett, like Coolidge,
chose not to run (also she needed the grade)—
but it wasn't much fun,

she could tell you,
hearing this man day after day sway the class
his Devilish way. So one night when curled fast asleep
under her duckdown quilt tippet, she got her thimble,
yarn, and colored thread,

made a soft little man
with a mouth all red, then without a peep
took her favorite hat pin, and stuck the fellow
stark dead.

After Hemingway

We left one morning the shores of Michigan
to find what we might
in Iowa City—
minutes past the fireflies
that feed upon the corn at night
we found Kenny's Bar,
where blue work shirts
and slender young girls
sat in their special prime,
serious and hurt,
eating out a strange heart
for rhyme.

Then
quite unexpectedly, a young
man, tall, bearded
since time began,
his hands blue as his shirt
and wrinkled
softly, stood up
full length to say, "I will not
be intimidated.
I will not,"
and then sat down to sigh
mournfully
between us.

Banal Story

Burt used to say to Eddie, "Hey, Polack!"—
and it really got the laughs because
Eddie had blond hair so curly
you had to wonder about it,
a girlish dimple in his chin,
big cherry red pimples, and
if he wasn't clumsy and thin
your old lady ate raw spinach.

Burt, on the other hand, had
a set of coal black
cut-down hopped-up stream-
lined lines,
a woman who did
the dirty deed extra-
special anytime, and he
never got pimples of any color.

Now Burt has four snotty kids,
the extra-special deed has run
to fat, and
his cut-down hopped-up stream-
lined lines seems slightly funny—
but when Eddie comes down
in his clean white shirt and gartered socks
to see what's what with the monkeys
and assembly jocks, guess what
Burt still sez to Eddie?

Poems

I sent my mother copies of my poems in print
to show her I was not a complete failure
and could do something besides
write dirty stories, and she was so happy

she replied with a poem of her own
about her heart waiting for spring and the beautiful
blue sky and some other lovelies
I don't remember, without calling it a poem

but you could tell that's what it was
because she lined it all out. The prettiest part
of her letter, however, was the end
where she said in her own true voice

"but mainly I can't wait for spring
because then my old man can get
to his garden and won't be bellyaching—
Oh he'll track in dirt and his hands

will never be clean and his breath
you can bet will be one big onion
once they get ripe, but it makes you
feel so good in your bones and it's all free!"

Four Vice Presidents

There were four learned Vice Presidents
running hither and thither one day to meet,
because the President, in a queer dither
himself, announced his retirement three years
early.

"Surely," they said, "we
must work intelligently to seek and interview
and reject and select he whom we most respect
academically."

So they tackled
the chore determinedly, forming Committee A to
seek, Committee B to interview, and Committees
C and D to reject and select—all perfectly
democratically.

Which took a little time,
and a little more time, and finally then some;
because, as the Chairman of Committee A said,
"Few are prime." The Chairman of Committee B
said, "Few indeed." And the Chairmen of
Committees C and D wholeheartedly agreed,
respectively.

"Why not,"
beamed one Vice President, "look for he whom
we most respect within our own splendid
academic family!" "Why not indeed!" beamed
a second, and the third and fourth beamed too,
enthusiastically.

So they realigned their chore and quietly began to pore over deserving possibilities from Liberal Arts, Medicine, Law, and Divinity.

Which didn't take much time at all, because the well-rounded Man wouldn't come from Divinity; Medicine was too conservative; Liberal Arts too liberal; and they distrusted men of Law unanimously.

So there they were, in dismal weather; finally, one Vice President ventured to say, "Why not elect one of us?" "Why not?" whispered a second, the third and fourth nodded very carefully, and all around the room four pairs of eyes turned inside out, surreptitiously.

Short Moral

When Elder Foxx, wed thirty years that night,
stood late behind his window looking at
the icicles that seemed like fragile bars
and saw (across the Square) the one who typed
his letters slip and fall—did he pick her up,
Dear Lord, and soothe her cool bruised knees and touch
his cheek to hers, climbing Mrs. Snyder's wicked stairs?
No, thank God, he turned around and found
the camphor sheets of Mrs. Foxx's proper bed.

Closing the Cottage

When last heard from I was
trying to get *be sweet*
to the last drop
into my mouth to get it
out, but her tall tan
was already up (against the fall

tide, that slight slip of white
where plastic tucks in flesh
sticking out) to take
the scratchy burlap curtains
down. It got me. Low,

I saw a single grain of sand
tilting on the secret bar
we'd built at night, rolling
nice and oiled into bed
to play our day's last
honest play. And knowing
she would have me

sweep it out to sea, I
didn't even have the heart
to make our joke
about her stretch undoing
millions. So
off I crawled, horny in
the lousy lizard's wind
that September.

Note from the Underground

In my novel I'm a slave to
down here under Mrs. Stella Skolnik
& her cabbage smell, my soul
is wasted—why?—why not!—
I'd like to know, five times a week
while people warm & snug can sleep
I get up! my skin's so mottled
listen, yogurt milk & half & half
cottage cheese with chives—anything!
I hock & eat it just to stay alive
for one more peek inside the Indian
chick from Sikkim's keyhole
(I would really like to understand
what makes her essence move!!) who lives
I counted sixteen pencil-lengths away
with him—a shaggy Polish beast
from Anthropology—and *that!*
is what keeps me the plot & Art
so thin and pretty much in bed
alone, God knows my flesh
can't get up strength enough
I need some meat to finish it.

Old Math on New Year's Eve

When the chairman of the math department
huffing and puffing like mad
blew his snaky whistle into the mouth
of the assistant professor's pretty wife
and the chairman's wife blew hers red-faced
into the side of the assistant professor's
head, the assistant professor calculating fast
rolled his eyes into three even lemons,
subtracted his tongue, and gave
undivided attention to his smile.

III

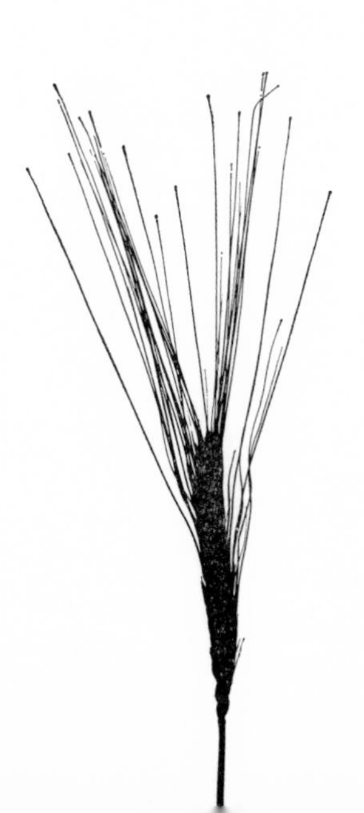

Nine Native Scenes

1
In Alaska, a Chilkat Indian, his stomach
rumbling, explains his native craft
to three white Brownies and a professional publicist,
who is out of sight, bored stiff, and too cold to smoke.

2
Last night on Belle Isle, a girl of sixteen,
a runaway, placed her cheeks against an old oak tree
whose roots lay out twisted, but solid in any
weather, and spoke the colors of her hungry soul.

3
In Oakland, in front of the bus depot,
a man in a long brown gown stands behind
a placard named "Alma Come Back." His toes appear
as neat red acorns, all in a row.

4
Opposite the Northland Nursing Home, a man and wife,
body to body, describe whole dreams.
Once, a flashing red light woke them, momentarily.
The snow, bone white, continues everywhere.

5
In Hartford, a teacher stays in a small room
with black cats and strange plants that grow
large in gray seasons. His peers wonder why.
Next year his superiors will not ask him back.

6
From a motor hotel in St. Paul: "We stayed
here last night. Took the packers till four A.M.
to finish. Ugh! Pat's baby boy was born dead
at four-thirty. She is *awfully* bad. Love, Corky."

7
In Des Moines, native ladies are gathered round
a room on laid-out comic strips and recipes
from the *Register* and *Tribune*. Busy as bees, they
learn the art of feeling wet naked plaster.

8
In Detroit, inside the bleak Grecian Gardens,
a black-eyed singer with ivory knees wiggles
her chunky fingers for Sobel, the artist who suffers
one wish: a dish of pressed duck to escape the routine.

9
Below my den, workmen chained to a manic saw
attack the dying elm. But that's the way
on this cheap street: you perform in the raw
circle of things, or lose.

American Gothic

A man taking a nap in Ishpeming, Michigan
is whacking off a goose's head. A woman,
working in her lap, is picking at
sixty years of loose thread. Two states away

their son, winning nix
at poker, whips out a pack of photos
that he bought in Mexico: he'll sell
the lot for fifty chips.

The dealer cuts the picture deck
and deals. His lady squeals:
"Why—their shoes and socks are on!"
"That," snaps another, rolling back

his lids, "is the obscenity." The son
collects. The man who's whacking off
a goose's head, the woman picking thread—
they hold their hands. Their hands are rough and red.

In the Orchard's Damp Grass

In the orchard's damp grass
behind the barn
a border collie broods.

You might have seen his eyes once
passing an empty house
in summer.

A killer of chickens, geese,
he won't admit to hang
his head.

Refuses even in this
fifth day to bend.
An old victim

tied round his neck
rots the fur,
secures his hate.

Song

O the woman in the "Song
of the Dog" by Degas

is open at the mouth
and big-busted above

two limp paws—

I had a woman once
who, combing all her hair down,

made a wall of touch
to music moving

fine as that.

In the Offices of Blue Cross/Blue Shield

The artist, a part-time janitor, is sweeping up
in front of the Medicare secretary staying overtime,
trying to get his work done before he dies
and so, head down, he doesn't notice
that her hands have abandoned the adding machine
to slip her left breast into the room,
nor that her eyes are on him and her lips
are on the verge of coming loose.

What he's doing is using his rouge sweeping compound
as acrylic and his broom as a brush,
and with a kissed Kleenex for focus
he's shaping just a body length
away from the Medicare secretary's cream-colored
straight-backed chair, a pair of passionate hips
which, come daybreak in his studio,
will lay for him rich beginnings.

The Drawings

This afternoon I saw the Lasansky Nazis hanging
high in their bones, in silence too close
to be easy in. That is the thing about human skin.

Slabs of hands grasping gaping holes,
a skull no different from my own—

I need this dark, these dry lips,
a sense of knowing there is nothing
more to say.

Pictures

I keep my pictures
in a box—beside our dog-
eared family Bible.

Name, birth, weight
and up-to-date death
data: these

and one thin clipping from my home-
town paper, saying
that I came back home, I've entered

in the record. Well,
here I am. Yesterday
I raked the leaves and mowed the grass,

sitting down. Science
is amazing. In appearance,
people say, I'm neat.

There's a girl I knew
who used that word
to bring out everything

she had. Today I'd stop her
on my knees. "Neat."
I operate with hooks

that cost an extra
breath—cheap
you might say.

Anyway
my pictures,
only one of which came out,

are both of me. In one
of course the kid
is cocky, smoking, posing—

the other shows the man
who came back home.

Tune

God bless the grass . . .
—Pete Seeger

It's a nice tune, Pete, but we are still
handing out hammers
to every man, woman, child and clawless dog
to use against the day
our eyes will finally slide
between the rocks
our prying fingers planted.

Happy Marriage

June bugs are banging
up against the screen—

and the woman, holding in,
holds back
the curtain of her window
with a yellow finger.

Down below, her man
has made his motorcycle
come alive, cool and firm
in tall blue riding boots.

Her eye hangs in smoke.

But four blood brothers,
gripping eagles in their pockets,
push in close
to see his moves are right.

She doesn't squirm, this Indian bitch,
she purrs—
she's got the classic lines, the stuff
to go.

No spark's been left too loose,
no gap to chance:
the form is strict,
the brothers keep it so.

They've got his knuckles for it
and his skin—

They've got the bones that she
who's counting cigarettes and hiding
from the moon
can never know.

Lady in the Ring

Rider of your bare back beast
riding tight to him your beast
your hair burning in the wind

if I took off my old skin
and hugged his ribs his lean
dancing in the ring

if I could press to him as you
press happy in your hips
prancing in the ring

if I could whisper to his neck
stroke his naked pace breathing
pulsing in the ring

I'd find a way to find my thighs
I'd find a way to raise them
from the darkness of the night.

The Trial

Betsy took two groups of rats
and kept their bellies full.
But to one she also gave her lips
in song, touched their flanks
and on occasion played them
warm, gay tricks to which
they responded by licking their paws.

For the second group she suffered
nothing gay—they stayed
in their dark cells
in the cellar, never knowing
her touch, her song, nor
the games she played.

In the end she nailed them all
to her laboratory wall,
and counted the time
by a special clock.
The unloved died soon, to a rat,
while the petted,
proving their will to endure,
held on, kicking for days.

Lovers at the Minor Key

Sitting opposite their ten
tapping fingers and
two mugs

of imported beer, the edgy lovers
(one of whom has
swollen feet,

the other does not
know it) suddenly
turn

to the bass player
biting down
hard

on his big black
cigar, as if
all

rhythm were pin-
pointed, stuck
in teeth.

B. F. Cassil-Jones

Along the cellar floor
of the West Branch Public Library,—
past questionable hard-
bounds, two forgotten
dust mops,
and the top to a
pint of gin thrown lately against all
the walls
of an impregnable life,—
B. F. Cassil-Jones follows
the trail home, knowing
that sin alone
can never do one in.

Encounter

When your first real love surprises you
after fifteen years on a dark street,
lets you feel the crow's-feet
beside her eyes, and then asks you

to look inside her hurt so fast
you recognize the empty whisky glass
and dreams with nails poking through—
how can you tell her you remember

only a party in Alice Bolt's basement
and her soft white cashmere breasts
dipping against your green corduroy
sportcoat, over and over and over?

IV

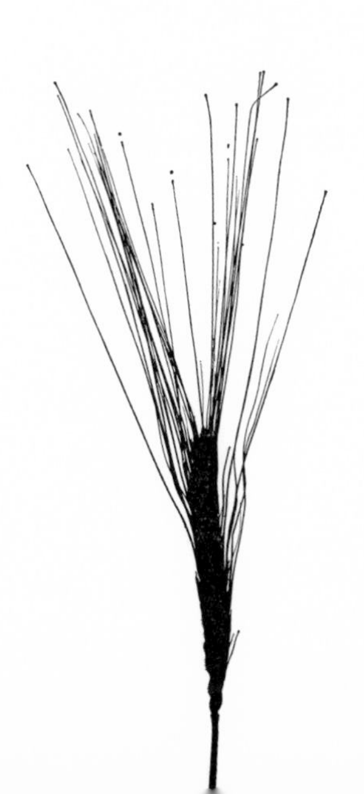

Edward

I knew him by a huge stomach laugh,
strange tumors on his arms,
and a Chippewa arrowhead he said he won
from the crafty Ojibway—in a turkey shoot
attended by many braves in bearskin.
I shuddered. My mother called him "Dutchman,"
baked him beans with sweet cuts of ham fat;
I learned he liked to watch her nurse me,—
his own sons had grown old too fast,
his daughters were too nervous.

Now I sniff his sons' cigar smoke, recall
he sent me with a dime to buy "one for you
and one for me"—there was an owl on the box.
I mixed the nails in his bins, learned
to swear "God damn to pot!"—and more,
which made my mother shudder.
Then we left to take another job.
His lumber yard could only hold two sons.

I look around his wood room, see
a single high-top boot, a tattered
True Detective. Will they use it,
whoever takes the place, to someday start a fire?
There are no relics of our trips to Gaylord.
I cannot smell the pine, nor find
on the magazine victim's yellow breasts
the blue, lusty eye that caught my first goshawk.
I hear the wind against the hill
his fat, protected deer fed at,
and perhaps the echo of a real wail
too far off—but nothing else below
the noisy time upstairs that matters.

Szostak

I list you from the past with food
I carry home in sacks, to keep me
going—nothing more. I lie of course

but that's the truth. You died
at one A.M.—reading Conrad
in the can by kerosene.

I write this straight, my friend,
as straight as you walked
home from Standish with your nightly pint

of whisky. Well, we waited
for the priest; wool trousers
made me itch; the hair

was trimmed above your lip. I recalled
that cake crumbs at a wedding
stuck in it—and how, when slicing up

a pig, you spit tobacco juice. Beyond
your head a satin pillow read
(in pink) "TO MY LOVING MOTHER";

under this a heart
(deep red) along which crawled a fly. Some fool
put pennies on your eyes. Assisted by the priest,

your wife knelt down, began her beads.
Her pretty nieces from Chicago followed, giving off
a cherry smell

that cured the kerosene. Old Pole,
I couldn't cry. That wasn't you. You'd been kicked
by mares, wore scars,

forked out shit. Secretly I scratched
my balls, then took the first slim silky pair
of legs I saw, and cooled us in your creek.

Rag Man

He moves in this old subdivision
—Indian Village—on toward
the Yacht Club like some turned
around Columbus, slowly rolling
over alley stones his wagon
that he fashioned and refashioned
nine times to keep it high
at such an angle only certain
love-struck schoolboys, birds,
or those bold sailors long dead
would understand—the river's
rich scent, gold, whatever else
he's just missed a hundred times
before, is really immaterial.

"Let's Hear from You!"

—Alumni News

Sir,
I am pleased to hear
that the Horticulture Plot is in full bloom
and that, even though my place has been taken
by 35,000 others, you still miss me.

As for your questionnaire,
it took me ten years
to rub the numbness half alive:
to sit all day and not plan
a "successful season."

The Dam

When
someone trapped
the buck beaver and
his mate left for good,
the pond
went down to muck
and then
it cracked—

occasional
moon craters
look up blankly
(like eye sockets
of dead frogs)
at twisted jack pine,
crucifixes
from an earlier time.

The Bastard Springer

The bastard springer, Spot,
tied with three kinds of knotted rope,
spends his hours lying in the matted dust
of a former chicken plot—
punishment for snapping
at a neighborhood stoning.

An Old Woman Speaks

At last my bones have turned on me
and lost I know
the sound they make. The sound
I play the clown
in white-face for.
In the morning.
Propped up against this skin
to drink a cup of weak tea and eat
my honey cake. Scented.
Dressed to kill.

Watching "Une Femme Mariée" Commit Adultery in the Basement of the Episcopal Church

& suddenly the folded chairs
won't work. It's pure French,
this smooth maneuvering
by the movie club, & heads

are blocking the language
of love. We want more
than just her thighs
filling up the screen, her

staring eyes—we need
to see, underneath the meeting
of their hands, the translation.
The lucky ones in front,

they sit still as silhouettes—
but we can't jockey
fast enough. Again
the reel takes the phrase

too soon—what did he say?—
& her lips
like private worship
only whisper . . .

V

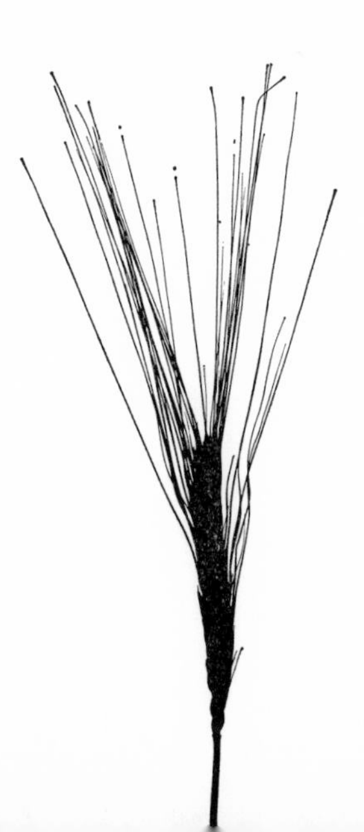

Under the Skylight

The fish she keeps (one-half burnished glass,
the other black as coal) kicked out
three quick wives at night
to flop to death. It's incompatible. Also,

notice that its home, a vase, is shaped
exactly like a bonnet. One might expect
some witty comment on it, yes?
No, the hairy man who handles two-bit actors

isn't interested
in fish—or glass bonnets. Nor the writer; he's
ill at ease, smoking menthol
cigarettes and drinking crème

de menthe on ice. His advice
is for her current work (a blue
clown playing chess): "Give his pieces
your blue face. Can't you

appreciate," he smiles, "the precious irony?"
Nodding yes, she keeps her brush
at rooks, kings, a queen.
He leaves too, at last; she'll change

the pace and do her nails. Mean-
while, the goldfish eats its castle.
Will it sleep then? And does it dream?
But now the one-time Prince of Yu-

goslavia is on the phone. Very
complimentary, he's also rather nice
to look at—not to mention very
married, too. But that's OK, he keeps

everything bright and humorous,
keeps for instance—Oh when all you see
at night is rain for instance—
the conversation light and clearly pretty.

The Sleepwalker

She thinks of something thin
and light, like wind in summer
hair, and rows of open windows
moving ribbons at the waist
of some secluded mistress,
up toward the cage she keeps
her blue, green love bird in,—
yet everything is night
and still, the moon has stopped
and turned to watch her
from a stark white
perch—she ought to think
about these things
—she hears it breathing
with her breathing,
with her one true
sunflower seed held out
and in the cage,
whose beak she now
in terror sees
she got dressed up
in skin to feed.

Letter to a Substitute Teacher

Dear Miss Miller,
You are someone
too sweet to sleep alone
and I can't help myself

sitting here hearing
your soft voice so
I must tell you
I like you

very much and would like
to know you better.
I know there is a difference
in our age and race

but we do have something
in common—You're a girl
and I'm a boy
and that is all

we need. Please
do not look at me
like I'm silly or sick
and most of all

please do not reject
my very first love
affair. If you do
not feel the same

as I do please
tell me how I can forget
your unforgettable voice
that reminds me

of Larry the Duke's pet
birds in the morning,
your blue eyes like the
Blessed Virgin's,

your golden hair and your
nice red mouth. Please
give me some sign
of how you feel,

I would rather be hurt
than forgotten forever.
Sincerely yours,
The Boy in the Green Shirt.

Poem

The girl who for years
could only smell and touch
the tissue of its petals

became aware one day
of what it was

and wept in the color
of her eyes.

To My Daughter

Not counting the little kids
you shock everyone you know
calling me Gary and Judy Judy
no one thinks it's natural
let alone healthy so we
better keep the pleasure
we get from filling your balloons
with water and squirting the dogs
when they come to lick us
in the tub, quiet, lover.

Wean Poem

The day my parents tried to wean me
not because it was the Depression certainly
but because I was going on three
their apartment house caught fire
and burned to the ground. I didn't
have anything to do with it naturally
(a man on relief was smoking in bed)

but my mother saved me and her ratty
muskrat coat by putting two and two together
and the next day at a relative's
my father, who is noted for his composure under stress,
broke out a bottle of Four Roses he couldn't afford
and more excited, I am told, than the day I was born
invited everybody in to have a drink with me.

For Judy

I was trying to write the perfect poem
having been rejected on the only decent
day that month—it didn't stink
and it didn't rain behind my eyes—

when, hanging out the clothes,
you turned and faced this failure—
waving the wind from your hair,
being the best of reasons.

Pitt Poetry Series

James Den Boer, *Learning the Way*
Jon Anderson, *Looking for Jonathan*
John Engels, *The Homer Mitchell Place*
Samuel Hazo, *Blood Rights*
David P. Young, *Sweating Out the Winter*
Fazıl Hüsnü Dağlarca, *Selected Poems*
Jack Anderson, *The Invention of New Jersey*
Gary Gildner, *First Practice*
David Steingass, *Body Compass*

COLOPHON

This book is composed entirely in Times Roman types, a face originally designed for the London *Times*. It was composed and printed by Heritage Printers, Inc., and bound in cloth from Holliston Mills. The book was designed by Gary Gore.